Maritsa Patrinos is a Brooklyn-based illustrator, writer, and comic artist. You may have seen her work for BuzzFeed, MTV, and Marvel, in the *New Yorker*, or just floating around on Instagram. Her work has been recognized by the Society of Illustrators, American Illustration, and the Ignatz Awards.

Library of Congress Cataloging-in-Publication Data:
Names: Patrinos, Maritsa, author, illustrator.
Title: Common blessings ; Common curses / Maritsa Patrinos.
Description: San Francisco : Chronicle Books, [2019]
Identifiers: LCCN 2018061299 | ISBN 9781452177960 (hardcover : alk. paper)
Subjects: LCSH: Life--Humor.
Classification: LCC PN6231.L48 P38 2019 | DDC 818/.602--dc23 LC record available at https://lccn.loc.gov/2018061299

ISBN: 978-1-4521-7796-0
Manufactured in China.

Artwork by Maritsa Patrinos.
Design by Maggie Edelman.

10 9 8 7 6 5 4 3 2 1

Chronicle Books LLC
680 Second Street
San Francisco, California 94107
www.chroniclebooks.com

COMMON
BLESSINGS
COMMON
CURSES

MARITSA PATRINOS

CHRONICLE BOOKS
680 SECOND STREET
SAN FRANCISCO, CA 94107
WWW.CHRONICLEBOOKS.COM

TRAFFiC

YOU LOST YOUR SNEEZE

PARALYZED BY INDECISION

DIDN'T CRY TODAY

ROOF ACCESS

THEY BUMP YOU UP
TO BUSINESS CLASS

THERE ARE ONLY
ENDPIECES LEFT

THE DRYER
EATS YOUR SOCKS

FOUND A TWENTY

YOU BURN YOUR
TONGUE ON PiZZA

YOU FIND THE
SQUISHY AVOCADOS

YOU HAVE 20/20 ViSiON

YOU LEAVE YOUR CREDIT
CARD AT THE BAR

YOU GET THE
BARTENDER'S ATTENTION

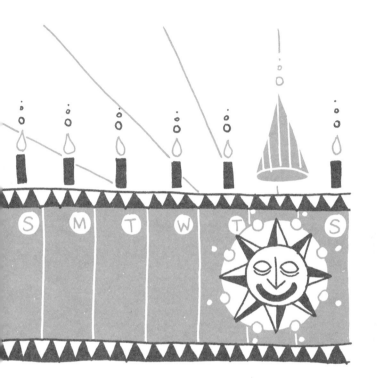

YOUR BIRTHDAY IS ON A FRIDAY

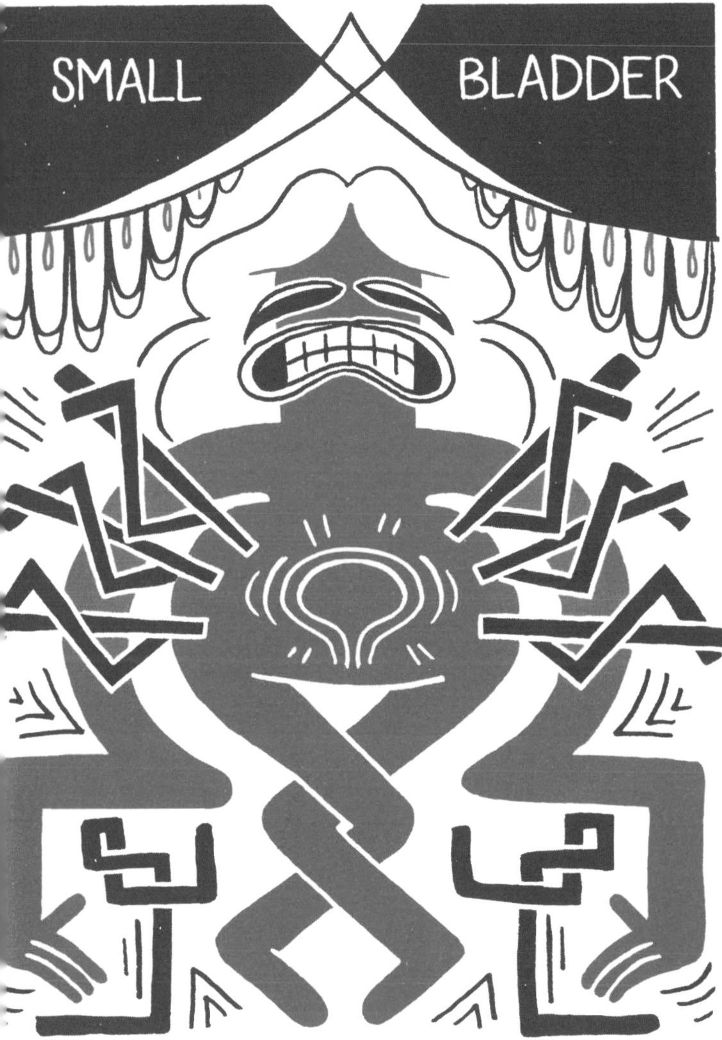
SMALL
BLADDER

FLAT TIRE

EMPTY THEATER

YOUR EX iS AT THE PARTY

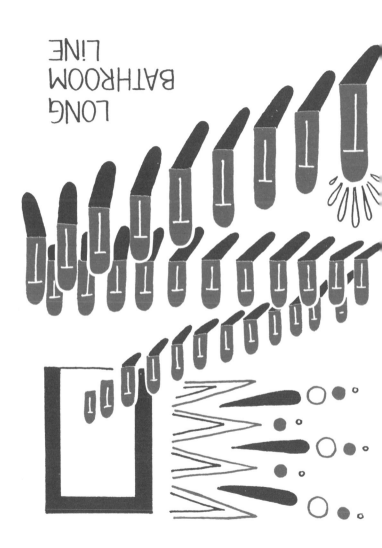

LONG
BATHROOM LINE

DOGS
LOVE YOU

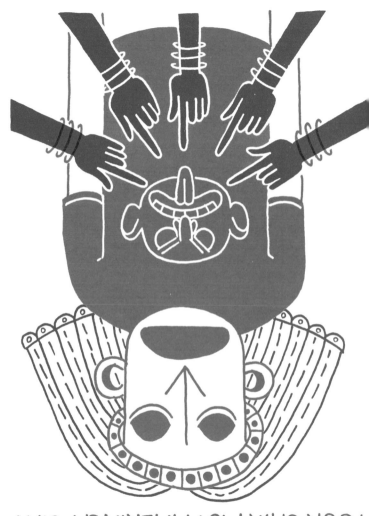

YOUR SHIRT iS A TALKiNG POiNT

GiFTED AT

FIRST iMPRESSIONS

GREEN THUMB

NO ONE NOTICED
YOUR HAIRCUT

NO SPICE TOLERANCE

GOOD HAIR DAY

FOUND A
PARKING SPOT

THE CHIP BAG IS HALF AIR

THEY FORGET TO CHARGE
YOU FOR THE GUAC

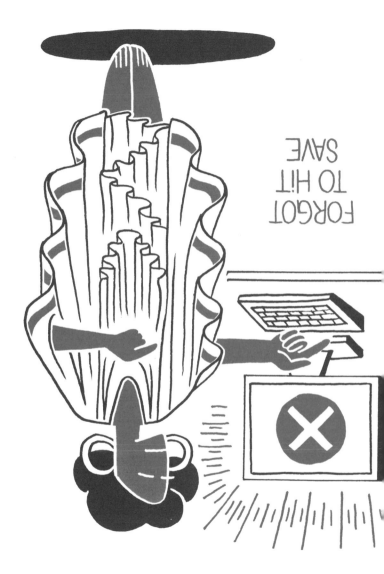

YOU KNOW HOW TO
GET THE KETCHUP OUT

GOT iN THE SHOWER
WiTH GLASSES ON

YOU HAVE ENOUGH CHANGE FOR LAUNDRY

I WENT TO THE SPAM FOLDER

MOSQUITOES DON'T LIKE YOUR BLOOD

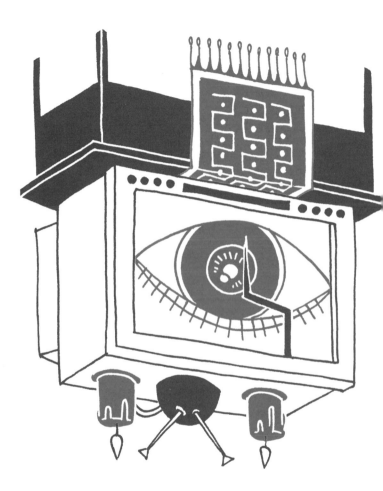

THE SERiES FiNALE SUCKED

SHE SMiLED AT YOU

YOU
LEFT YOUR
HEADPHONES
AT HOME

NO ONE HEARD YOU FART

YOU'RE THERE TO SIGN
FOR YOUR PACKAGE

YOU MAKE EYE CONTACT FROM
INSIDE BATHROOM STALLS

YOU ALWAYS WAKE UP

IN TIME FOR YOUR STOP

UTILITIES ARE INCLUDED

YOU CUT YOUR NAILS TOO SHORT

HUNG OVER AT THE DENTIST

EiGHT HOURS SLEEP

COMMON BLESSINGS
COMMON CURSES

MARITSA PATRINOS

CHRONICLE BOOKS
680 SECOND STREET
SAN FRANCISCO, CA 94107
WWW.CHRONICLEBOOKS.COM

Maritsa Patrinos is a Brooklyn-based illustrator, writer, and comic artist. You may have seen her work for BuzzFeed, MTV, and Marvel, in the *New Yorker*, or just floating around on Instagram. Her work has been recognized by the Society of Illustrators, American Illustration, and the Ignatz Awards.

Library of Congress Cataloging-in-Publication Data:
Names: Patrinos, Maritsa, author, illustrator.
Title: Common blessings ; Common curses / Maritsa Patrinos.
Description: San Francisco : Chronicle Books, [2019]
Identifiers: LCCN 2018061299 | ISBN 9781452177960 (hardcover : alk. paper)
Subjects: LCSH: Life--Humor.
Classification: LCC PN6231.L48 P38 2019 | DDC 818/.602--dc23 LC record available at https://lccn.loc.gov/2018061299

ISBN: 978-1-4521-7796-0
Manufactured in China.

FSC
www.fsc.org
MIX
Paper
FSC® C136333

Artwork by Maritsa Patrinos.
Design by Maggie Edelman.

10 9 8 7 6 5 4 3 2 1

Chronicle Books LLC
680 Second Street
San Francisco, California 94107
www.chroniclebooks.com